# Conter

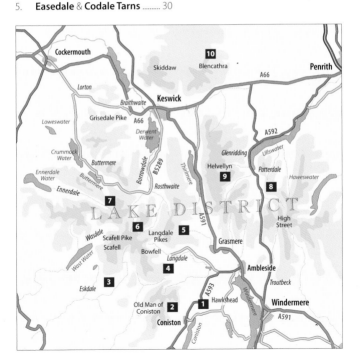

## England's Largest National Park

THE LAKE DISTRICT NATIONAL PARK is the largest and most popular of the thirteen National Parks in England and Wales. Created as one of Britain's first National Parks in 1951, its role is to 'conserve and enhance' the natural beauty, wildlife and culture of this iconic English landscape, not just for residents and visitors today but for future generations, too.

Remarkably, the National Park contains every scrap of England's land over 3,000 feet, including its highest mountain, Scafell Pike. Packed within the Park's 885 square miles are numerous peaks and fells, over 400 lakes and tarns, around 50 dales, six National Nature Reserves, and more than 100 Sites of Special Scientific Interest—all publicly accessible on over 1,800 miles of footpaths and other rights of way. It's no surprise then, that the Lake District attracts an estimated 15 million visitors a year.

*Dawn over Tarn Hows*

## Lake District Tarns

Norsemen, who dominated Lakeland 1,000 years ago, called the small bodies of water they found in the mountains *tjorns*—'little lakes' or , literally, 'teardrops'. Now known as tarns, they are remnants of the last Ice Age when huge ice sheets scoured out hollows in the mountains that then filled with water.

There are hundreds of tarns in the National Park: from tiny pools sparkling like blue jewels on high, lonely ridge tops, to small lakes sitting cold and moody at the base of sombre cliffs.

"Beneath our feet, a little lowly vale...
A liquid pool that glittered in the sun,
... Ah! what a sweet Recess, thought I, is here."

William Wordsworth, *The Excursion*, 1814

# TOP **10** Walks: Walks to Tarns

THERE ARE LITERALLY HUNDREDS of tarns scattered throughout the Lake District, each with its own special character. The ten in this book have been chosen for their moody locations, their dramatic backdrops, and the superb walks to get to them. Some are enclosed within high mountain combs, while others are cradled on low-lying hills; some are en-route to popular summits, others are off the beaten track. Yet each of them will provide walkers with memories to cherish for a lifetime.

Tarn Hows — page 8

Levers Water — page 14

...tony & Eel Tarns — page 18

...lea Tarn — page 24

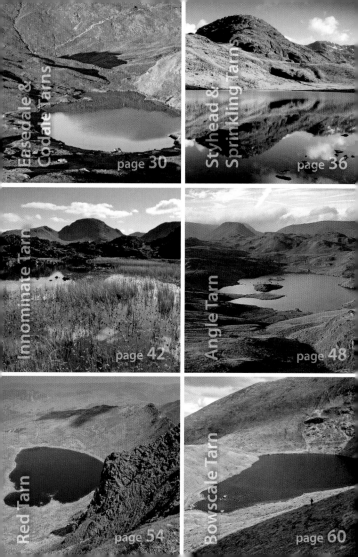

*Tarn Hows*

# Tarn Hows

*A gentle saunter through undulating woods to one of Lakeland's most popular beauty spots*

**What to expect:**

*Field and woodland paths, some tracks*

**Distance/time:** 9.5km/6 miles. Allow 2½-3 hours

**Start:** Pay and Display car park beside the Tourist Information Centre in the centre of Coniston

**Grid ref:** SD 303 975

**Ordnance Survey Map:** OL 7 *The English Lakes South-eastern area Windermere, Kendal and Silverdale*

**After the walk:** Pubs, cafés and tearooms in Coniston

### Walk outline

*Starting from Coniston, this straightforward walk follows a series of paths across fields and through woods to the beautifully situated Tarn Hows. A constructed track does a circuit of this delightful body of water, after which the route descends beside the pretty cascades of Tom Gill. A series of farm paths, woodland trails and quiet lanes then returns the walker to Coniston.*

### Tarn Hows

Despite being man-made, Tarn Hows is well worth a visit. There used to be three tiny tarns here, but the single body of water you see today was created when the 19th-century industrialist James Marshall dammed one of them. With plans based on ideas of the 'picturesque' that were popular at the time, he wanted to create something beautiful. In so doing, he also planted the conifers surrounding the tarn, a feature that is intended both to frame and dramatically reveal views of his creation.

*Tom Gill*

*Waterlily*

**Winter glow:** *The final rays from a winter sunset illuminate the slopes of Tom Heights*

## The Walk

**1.** From the car park entrance go ahead across 'Ruskin Avenue' and turn right along the road (Tilberthwaite Avenue). Follow the road to the edge of **Coniston** and immediately before a bridge, turn left into 'Shepherds Bridge Lane'. Follow the lane with the beck to your right and, opposite the primary school, take the signed footpath over the bridge on the right. Immediately after the bridge turn left along the bank to enter fields.

The path heads off across the field passing beneath a line of oaks and towards a stone-built folly.

*This Gothic construction is probably the grandest and most fanciful kennel you will ever see. It was built by James Marshall, who was also responsible for the creation of Tarn Hows, after he became master of the Coniston foxhounds in 1839.*

The path continues beside the folly on a gentle rise towards woods. Enter the woods by a kissing gate surrounded by ancient yew trees and walk ahead through the trees to enter fields again.

Follow the obvious path ahead through a large field and at the far end bear left to go through a gate. The path cuts directly through the next field aiming for a kissing gate in the far fence. This leads onto a farm track. Turn left along the track.

**2.** Follow the track to the old stone bridge but don't cross the bridge, instead, go through the small foot gate into the field directly ahead (signed to 'Tarn Hows'). Walk across the field to enter woods again by a kissing gate adjacent to **Yewdale Beck**. The path keeps beside the beck briefly, before veering right-wards to begin a gentle climb through the trees.

At the upper edge of the woods the path runs beside a wall and there are good views left across the valley into Yewdale.

Go through two gates ahead to reach the access road to a small cottage on the left. Turn right and follow the access road to a tarmac lane.

**3.** Turn left and walk up the lane to **Tarn Hows**.

*Hidden from view until the last moment, Tarn Hows sits in a hollow surrounded by woods and low-lying fells. To the west, Wetherlam and the Coniston fells provide a craggy backdrop to the delightful scene.*

**Morning calm:** *A view across Tarn Hows to Wetherlam and the Coniston fells*

As the lane swing right, bear left onto a footpath which leads around the tarn in an anti-clockwise direction.

**4.** Immediately before the path crosses the outflow, take the signed footpath on the right ('Glen Mary, Yew Tree Tarn'). This hugs the rocky side of the beck which steepens into a series of picturesque cascades. The climax is **Tom Gill Waterfall,** a modest affair by Lakeland standards, set amid oak woods.

**5.** As you approach the road turn left over a footbridge and walk left through a small car park. At the end of the car park a permissive path enters fields to run parallel to the road. Almost opposite **Yew Tree Farm** on the right, go through the kissing gate on the right, cross the road and bear right to the farm access road.

**6.** Take the signed permissive bridleway to the right of the farm. At a fork ignore a path on the right continuing ahead on the well-made gravel surface.

**7.** At a narrow lane turn left over the little stone bridge, then bear right immediately on the bridleway which continues parallel to the road. Cross the

Tilberthwaite lane and continue through woods below **Yewdale Fells** (2km).

**8.** Leave the woods by a small gate in the wall ahead and in 150 metres go left through a second gate. Walk down to the lane and turn right. At the next junction turn left, then immediately right into **Shepherds Bridge Lane**. Retrace the outward route to complete the walk. ♦

### Monk Coniston estate

*Tarn Hows is part of the Monk Coniston estate bought by James Marshall in 1835. In 1926, the hall and gardens were sold to John Bradshaw. Beatrix Potter bought the rest of the estate, including Tarn Hows, in 1930. She then sold half at cost price to the National Trust; the other half passed to the charity after her death in 1943. The National Trust reunited the estate in 1945 by purchasing the hall and gardens.*

*Cloud over Levers Water*

# Levers Water

*A moderate walk up to a glacial basin at the craggy base of the Coniston fells*

**What to expect:**
*Beckside path, old mine tracks and gentle descent*

**Distance/time:** 7km/4½miles. Allow 2½-3½ hours

**Start:** Main Pay and Display car park near the Tourist Information Centre in Coniston

**Grid ref:** SD 303 975

**Ordnance Survey Map:** OL 6 *The English Lakes North-western area. Coniston, Ulverston & Barrow-in-Furness*

**After the walk:** Wide choice of pubs and cafés in Coniston

## Walk outline

*This walk makes use of miners' tracks in the Coppermines Valley. The route is reasonably straightforward, although the path leading away from Levers Water and into the magnificent Boulder Valley can be a little hard to find, and some of the tracks can be annoyingly stony at times. There are one or two moderately steep climbs, but these are short-lived.*

## Levers Water

Levers Water sits glittering in a glacial bowl at the foot of the Coniston fells. It started life as a natural tarn, although it was dammed and enlarged to provide water for the mines. Its status today as a reservoir though doesn't detract from the grandeur of its setting.

*Coppermines Valley*

The walk passes through a landscape dotted with the remains of Coniston's ancient copper mining industry. While industrial archaeology enthusiasts marvel at how the German miners of the 16th- and 17th-centuries managed to work the seams before the days of Victorian engineering, others will be spellbound by the craggy fells on all sides.

*Meadow pipit*

## The Walk

**1.** Leave the car park, turn left along the residential road and left along the B5285. At the T-junction, turn left again, then take the road on the right. Turn right along the lane after the Sun Hotel. Go through the gate at the top to access a rough track that soon climbs alongside **Church Beck**.

**2.** Cross the beck via **Miners Bridge** and turn left to continue upstream. Follow the track as it passes in front of the **Coppermines Youth Hostel** (formerly the old mine office) and then climbs beside a waterfall. When the track forks about 400 metres beyond the hostel, bear right. (You will see the water treatment works just down to your left here.) Almost immediately, turn right up a grassy path, which

provides a brief but welcome respite from the stony track. This soon swings left as it joins a path coming in from the right. Continue uphill on rejoining the main track.

**3.** When you finally reach **Levers Water**, turn left to cross the dam. Follow the water's edge for a short while and then bear left at a fork in the path—up towards some fenced workings.

This dangerous area is known as the **Back Strings** and forms part of the original copper workings by the German miners.

**4.** Immediately after a second fenced area, turn left to head up the slope, at first with the fence on your left. You will soon pick up a clearer path that takes you down into **Boulder Valley** at the foot of **Brim Fell**'s steep eastern slopes. After crossing a bridge over **Low Water Beck**, you pass a huge boulder known as the **Pudding Stone**.

0    1km    1 mile

© Crown copyright and/or database right. All rights reserved. License number 100047867

**Grand setting:** *Levers Water started life as a natural tarn but was enlarged by miners*

**5.** Turn left at a T-junction and then, almost immediately, bear left along the lower of the two tracks. You will eventually see **Church Beck** again down to your left. Keep left at a fork in the path near **Miners' Bridge**, but don't cross the bridge. From here it's simply a case of retracing your steps to the car park, remembering to turn left at the Sun Hotel, left at the T-junction and then immediately right at **St Andrew's Church**, to complete the walk. ♦

## Coppermines Valley

*There is evidence of copper mining in Coniston as far back as 1599, soon after German miners were invited to England by Elizabeth I. Employed by the Company of Mines Royal, they established copper and lead mines throughout Cumbria. Most of the workings passed on this walk date from the 19th century, but the remains of earlier mines, including the Back Strings (left), can be seen near Levers Water.*

*Eel Tarn with Harter Fell in the background*

# Stony & Eel Tarns

*A walk to two secret tarns in one of the Lake District's quietest and most beautiful valleys*

**What to expect:**
*Farm paths and tracks; open fell, sometimes boggy*

**Distance/time:** 8km/5 miles. Allow 2½-3 hours

**Start:** Dalegarth Station, Eskdale—the terminus of the La'al Ratty railway

**Grid ref:** NY 173 007

**Ordnance Survey Map:** OL 6 *The English Lakes South-western area. Coniston, Ulverston & Barrow-in-Furness*

**After the walk:** The Boot Inn and the Brook House Inn in Boot; Fellbites Café at Dalegarth Station

## Walk outline

*After a short section of road walking, the route leaves Boot and heads out over farmland, crossing several unusual stiles. On reaching the open fell, compass and map-reading skills will be put to the test as the paths are sometimes vague and boggy. Stony Tarn is visited first and then a slightly clearer path drops walkers down to Eel Tarn. Finally, a fell track and quiet lane lead back to Boot.*

## Stony Tarn and Eel Tarn

Stony Tarn and Eel Tarn are hidden away in a secluded part of Eskdale. Few walkers frequent this peaceful area of low-lying crags and damp moorland to the north-east of Boot. But wandering up and over the rocky outcrops and in between the grassy knolls, with a new view at every turn, makes for a lovely excursion.

Walkers will stumble upon Stony Tarn first, hidden from view until the last moment by surrounding crags. Eel Tarn, on the other hand, is visible long before you reach it— spreading out over flat moorland where cattle graze.

*Descending to Eel Tarn*

*Red darter dragonfly*

## The Walk

**1.** Leave the station and turn left along the road and left again at the **Brook House Inn**—towards 'Boot'. Just before the humpback bridge at the end of the road, turn right—along a track beside a cottage.

**2.** Climb gently for 120 metres beside **Whillan Beck** and then go through the squeeze stile on the right. The path passes through a kissing-gate and then a larger gate around the back of the **Hollins Farm** campsite. Maintaining the same line, walk between the farmhouse on the left and the camping barn on the right. You then pick up a waymarked path heading out of the farmyard and garden.

Cross the stile in the wall and then keep close to the wall on your right. A couple of gated stiles enable walkers

to cross two unusually wide walls. Two more stiles then lead onto a vehicle track, along which you turn left. After passing a farmhouse on the left, go through a kissing-gate on the right. The right-of-way follows the line of the wall over to the left at first and then goes through a gap in another wall about 50 metres to the right of a cottage. (The gap has white arrows painted on it.) Swing right and then left, as indicated by the waymarker. Go through the gate and turn right.

**3.** Walk along the track for 80 metres, passing a large shed on the left, and then go through a gate on the left. A faint, grassy path climbs gently beside the wall on your left and

0            1km
½ mile

**Hidden away:** *Stony Tarn is one of Eskdale's best-kept secrets*

leads up to a gate. Once through this, turn right along a path winding its way uphill. Once over the ladder stile at the top of this bracken-filled enclosure, turn right alongside the wall.

**4.** Watch carefully for the next turning. As the path descends through a wide gap between the wall on your right and another coming down from the left, it crosses a boggy area. Almost immediately, turn sharp left (north-east) along an easy-to miss path, so that the

wall that was on your left is now on your right.

The path soon swings away from the wall and dissolves in the bog. Keep to the right of the damp ground and then climb the slope ahead, alongside a short stretch of low wall (north-north-east). You should pick up a faint path on the ground at the top of this damp ground. It skirts the left of the next boggy area and continues north-north-east through a gap between the hills. Pass about 100 metres to the left of a tiny waterfall, partly hidden by small trees. Beyond

**Evening glory:** *A beautiful summer's evening at Eel Tarn*

the falls, keep left at a faint fork (north-north-east). You will see a beck, Stony Tarn's outlet stream, down to your right. The path climbs the flank of the hill and then drops to the beck. Cross the water and follow the channel upstream—to the edge of **Stony Tarn**.

**5.** Recross the outlet stream and head up the bracken-covered slope to the north. About 80 metres above the water, turn left along a path close to a small sheepfold. On reaching a clearer path, turn left again. This winds its way down

to **Eel Tarn**, disappearing into the mire from the time to time. If you should lose it, the general direction is southwest.

The path passes around the northeast side of the tarn, keeping some way back from the water's edge. A wooden pole indicates the way across a boggy area.

**6.** Having passed the tarn, ignore the path heading left; continue west, across damp, pathless ground and down beside the outlet stream. You quickly reach a clear track, along which you turn left. This later passes between two drystone walls. As the Brook House Inn comes into view below, watch for a fingerpost down to the right—at a point

where the wall kinks right. The track bypasses the signpost, so if you miss it, you will miss your turning. Drop to the fingerpost and turn right, through a gate.

**7.** Turn left along the track to drop back into **Boot**. Turn left at the road and right at the **Brook House Inn** to return to **Dalegarth Station** to complete the walk. ♦

### Peat

*Look up onto the fells as you descend into Boot at the end of the walk and you will see some 18th-century stone peat huts. Eskdale once relied heavily on peat for fuel. After cutting and leaving it to dry on the moor for several weeks, local families would transport it to the huts by horse-drawn sledge where it would be stored until it was needed in the winter.*

*Blea Tarn and the Langdale Pikes at first light*

# Blea Tarn

*A short, but steep walk onto a low, rocky fell towered over by iconic Langdale peaks*

**What to expect:**
*Fell paths, including a
narrow rock squeeze;
tarn-side track*

**Distance/time:** 4.5km/3 miles. Allow 2-2½ hours

**Start:** National Trust's Blea Tarn Pay and Display car park

**Grid ref:** NY 295 043

**Ordnance Survey Map:** OL 6 *The English Lakes South-western area. Coniston, Ulverston & Barrow-in-Furness*

**After the walk:** Old Dungeon Ghyll Hotel in Great Langdale

## Walk outline

*A steep, but mostly grassy path climbs to the 467-metre top of Lingmoor Fell. With fantastic views ahead, the route then follows the superb ridge. A rocky path hugs Side Pike's main buttress and passes through a narrow squeeze. After a short detour to the 344 metre summit, a faint path drops to the road. A constructed track then skirts Blea Tarn.*

## Blea Tarn

Photographers adore Blea Tarn. Poised with camera and tripod at the water's edge, they wait for the ideal moment to capture an image of this beautiful tarn with its immaculate backdrop. The bowl in which the tarn sits is gorgeous in itself—lightly wooded and with steep slopes to the east and west—but it is the Langdale Pikes, perfectly framed in the gap created by Blea Tarn Pass, that make this scene so idyllic.

*Bleatarn House*

This short but immensely satisfying walk heads onto the high ground to the east of the tarn, providing excellent views of the water below and the mountains ahead.

*Fox*

## The Walk

**1.** Turn right out of the car park. Walk along the road for almost 300 metres and then take a faint path climbing through the bracken on your right. This heads towards a steep-sided gill, just before which it joins a clearer path coming up from the left. (If you should miss the initial turning off the road, continue a little further and then, just before you reach the whitewashed cottage of **Bleatarn House**, you will see a wall to the right of the road. Take the path climbing alongside this.) Whichever way you come off the road, follow the beck upstream, passing through a gap in a wall on the climb.

*As you ascend, take some time to pause and enjoy the stunning mountain scenery: Wetherlam and Swirl How are over to the right; behind you, Crinkle Crags, Bowfell and the Langdale Pikes are clearly visible; and, all the while, Blea Tarn is down to the right.*

**2.** Cross the stile in the next wall you encounter and continue uphill with the wall on your immediate left. The path is rough and stony, but it's not long before you reach the ridge. Cross the stile in the fence and turn left to climb quickly to the cairn. This is **Brown How**, the highest point of Lingmoor Fell.

*The outstanding views now also include the Helvellyn range, Fairfield, Windermere, the Pennines and Morecambe Bay.*

**3.** Head downhill with the dilapidated wall/fence on your left and the mountains of **Langdale** straight ahead. Blea Tarn puts in an appearance far below from time to time as does Lingmoor Tarn, lying forgotten in the folds of the fell down to the right. There is a long drop to Side Pike and the path is steep and rocky in

0            1km
        ½ mile

**Setting sun:** *The Langdale Pikes towards the end of the walk*

places. It forks at a distinct left-hand kink in the fence. Take either route here: before too long, the right-hand path swings back round to the wall/fence, which continues to be your faithful companion, guiding you down some rough ground.

*Drystone walls, such as the one snaking along this lovely ridge, are an integral part of Lakeland. The walls are built on a foundation of two parallel rows of large boulders on either side of a trench. The sides are then built up and the inside is filled with smaller stones. At regular intervals, a layer of 'through stones' is placed across the width of the wall to strengthen it. Walls are generally topped with a row of slanting stones, known as 'cam-stones', to discourage sheep from climbing them.*

**4.** With the worst of the descent behind you, cross a stile in the wall on your left and continue downhill with the wall now on your right. This path takes you all the way to the base of **Side Pike's** formidable buttresses, straight ahead.

**Mirror image:** *The Langdale Pikes form the perfect backdrop to Blea Tarn*

Go through a kissing-gate in a fence and then continue up towards the steep rock face. Only as you reach the base of the crag does the path finally swing left to find a route around the southern side of the fell. It clings tightly to a ledge and squeezes its way through a narrow gap between the rocks. The path then swings right and climbs.

**5.** Just after the Langdales reappear, the path splits. Bear right for the short, easy climb to the summit of **Side Pike**, but the main route heads left. Follow the wall on your right until the path goes through a gap in it. With the ground ahead suddenly dropping away steeply, the route is unclear. Basically, you need to pick up a path, cairned in places, that negotiates several shallow rocky ledges to descend in a mostly west-south-west direction. Nearing the base of the fell, this goes through one kissing-gate and then another, providing access to the road at **Blea Tarn Pass**.

**6.** Cross straight over and then, a few metres back from the road, go through the gate on the left to access a constructed path.

*This is one of the Lake District National*

*Park's 'Miles Without Stiles' route—paths specially constructed for people with mobility problems. Sections of this one are suitable for people operating their own wheelchairs.*

Before long, you have **Blea Tarn** on your left. At a T-junction, turn left to cross the footbridge over the outlet stream. This path comes out at the road opposite the car park to complete the walk. ♦

### Old Dungeon Ghyll

*The Old Dungeon Ghyll Hotel, owned by the National Trust since 1929, was known as Middlefell Inn at the end of the 19th century. Back then, horse-drawn coaches would bring visitors from Little Langdale over Blea Tarn Pass. They would stop at the top and blow their horn, a signal to get lunch or tea ready—the number of blasts informed the staff of the number of passengers requiring a meal.*

*Easdale Tarn and Blea Crag*

# Easedale & Codale Tarns

*Two tarns—one popular with visitors, one hidden away;
and a visit to lonely Tarn Crag*

**What to expect:**

*Clear paths as far as
Codale Tarn, then open
fell; one rocky section*

**Distance/time:** 11km/7 miles. Allow 3-4 hours

**Start:** The beginning of the Easedale Road in Grasmere village—
opposite the Sam Read bookshop

**Grid ref:** NY 337 076

**Ordnance Survey Map:** OL 6 *The English Lakes South-western area.
Coniston, Ulverston & Barrow-in-Furness;* and OL 7 *The English Lakes
South-eastern area. Windermere, Kendal & Silverdale*

**After the walk:** Various pubs and cafés in Grasmere

### Walk outline

*A well trodden path climbs beside the dramatic waterfalls of
Sourmilk Gill to beautiful Easedale Tarn. Continuing further
into the valley, the next target is Codale Tarn. A final grassy
climb leads onto Tarn Crag, the highest and loneliest part of
the walk. Paths are, at best, vague here. The route drops down
a bracken-covered ridge and into Far Easedale where a good
track leads back to Grasmere.*

### Easedale Tarn and Codale Tarn

Easedale Tarn has long been admired by visitors: in
Victorian times, there was even a refreshments hut at
the water's edge, serving light lunches and hot drinks.
Its popularity is hardly surprising: it is situated in a lovely
location 200 metres above Grasmere with steep slopes to
the north and south-west.

Codale Tarn, tucked into a quiet hollow in the fells below
Codale Head, is another story. Equally attractive, but
another 180 metres higher up the valley, there's a bit more
effort required to reach it. Fewer people venture this far.

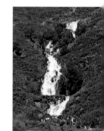

*Sourmilk Gill waterfalls*

*Common frog*

## The Walk

**1**. From the centre of **Grasmere**, walk along Easedale Road for nearly 700 metres until you see a small footbridge in the trees to your left. Cross this bridge—signposted 'Easedale Tarn'—and then a second, smaller bridge. Keep to the clear, beckside track until it goes through a gate.

**2**. Beyond this, cross the farm track and keep straight ahead on a narrower path —a signpost, partly hidden in a holly bush on the right, shows the way. After a gate, the more sustained climbing begins—on a constructed path running alongside a drystone wall and then beside the tumultuous waterfalls of **Sourmilk Gill**.

**3**. On reaching **Easedale Tarn**, follow the main path as it skirts the southern side of the tarn and then begins to climb. The path is steep in places and you may need to use your hands for balance as you clamber up the bare rock just below **Belles Knott**. The gradient eventually eases as you reach a more open area.

**4**. Leave the main path here by turning right along a narrow trail that quickly drops to cross the beck and continues to **Codale Tarn**. The path skirts the water's edge before crossing the outlet stream and then continuing to the northern end of the tarn.

**5**. There are few obvious routes on the ground from now on, but there are some faint paths and, as long as you know how to use a map and compass, you shouldn't go wrong. Just before

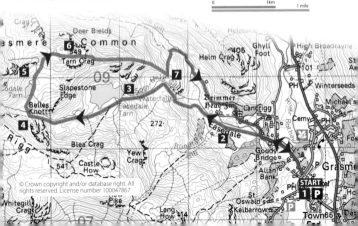

**Autumn light:** *Looking down to Easedale Tarn from Belles Knott*

reaching the inlet stream, bear right (north-east) away from the tarn. There is a faint path on the ground that runs parallel with the inlet stream—about 80 metres to the right of it, avoiding the boggy ground closer to the beck.

As you draw level with a sheepfold off to your left, you climb more steeply, now heading north up the grassy slope. On reaching the base of some craggier ground at the top of this rise, bear right (north-east) along a faint path skirting the rocky area to your left. Do not be tempted by the clearer path that swings left towards Codale Head. You quickly reach a faint crossing of paths where you turn right.

**6.** Just before the path starts dropping away more steeply, you will see a faint path off to the left. Take this for a quick detour onto the 485 metre summit of **Tarn Crag**.

*Fairfield and the Helvellyn range dominate the scene to the north-east, but all eyes will inevitably be drawn to the charming view down Easedale and on to Grasmere.*

**Green bowl:** *Easedale Tarn rests in a lovely location 200 metres above Grasmere*

To continue on the route, drop back to the main path and then head steeply down a shallow, mostly grassy gully. Walkers' boots have created a faint zig-zagging path that will ease your descent. At the bottom of this first drop, continue east along the faint, grassy ridge path. Don't be tempted by clearer paths heading off down to the right—although the worst that could happen would be that you'd end up back at Easedale Tarn. There are no right and wrong ways of descending this lonely ridge. There are faint paths all over

the place—some stick to the highest ground; some avoid the craggiest bits. It's a case of pick and mix. Choose the options that suit you best—and enjoy! In its lower stages, the ridge path descends through bracken.

**7.** On reaching a T-junction with a clearer path, turn left. You are unlikely to go wrong here—the route is obvious, there are yellow waymarkers to guide you and, just in case you are in any doubt, there is a huge boulder with 'Grasmere' and a large arrow painted on it.

**8.** Approaching the valley bottom in **Far Easedale**, veer right where a path

joins from the left. Cross the wooden footbridge and head downstream. You eventually lose the beck, but the way ahead is obvious. At a junction of tracks, keep straight ahead—signposted for 'Grasmere'. Go through the gate and walk down the lane. Swing left along the asphalt and follow the road back into **Grasmere village** to complete the walk. ♦

### 'The Black Quarter'

*It's hard to escape from references to the Wordsworths in and around Grasmere—and Easedale Tarn is no exception. William and his sister Dorothy were frequent visitors to the tarn. They referred to the valley as 'the Black Quarter', claiming it was the source of all the bad weather that hit Grasmere. The Wordsworths lived in Grasmere for many years.*

*Styhead Tarn and Great End*

# Styhead & Sprinkling Tarns

*A moderate walk beneath some of Lakeland's highest and most impressive mountains*

**What to expect:**

*Well-walked tracks and paths throughout, loose on the initial descent*

**Distance/time:** 9km/5½ miles. Allow 3-4 hours

**Start:** Seathwaite in Borrowdale. The roadside parking leading to Seathwaite fills up early. Walkers may need to park in the National Trust Pay and Display car park in Seatoller, 2 kilometres away

**Grid ref:** N Y235 123

**Ordnance Survey Map:** OL 7  *The English Lakes North-western area. Keswick, Cockermouth & Wigton;* and OL 6 *The English Lakes South-western area. Coniston, Ulverston & Barrow-in-Furness*

**After the walk:** Yew Tree Country Restaurant in Seatoller

## Walk outline

*Easy walking on a stony track beside Grains Gill leads to the Styhead Gill path. After a moderate ascent beside Taylorgill Force and then alongside the beck, the first of the tarns—Styhead Tarn—is reached. More climbing on a well-used track beneath Great End's mighty buttresses leads to Sprinkling Tarn. The long descent is via Ruddy Gill and Grains Gill. The path is badly eroded in places.*

## Styhead Tarn and Sprinkling Tarn

It's hard to match these two tarns for the drama and grandeur of their settings. Styhead Tarn sits at the base of the iconic Great Gable, with the fearsome eastern face of Lingmell dominating the scene. Get here early or late in the day, and there's a good chance there will be tents pitched beside the water, wild-campers enjoying some of the most spectacular mountain scenery in England.

Higher still, Sprinkling Tarn is renowned for being the wettest place in the country. Great End's mighty buttresses loom over this majestic body of water.

*Stockley Bridge*

*Foxglove*

**Popular path:** *The Styhead Gill path is used by walkers aiming for Scafell Pike*

## The Walk

**1.** Having parked on the Seathwaite road, walk south and follow the track into the farmyard and out the other end.

*As you make your way up the valley on a clear, broad track, the slopes on your right belong to Base Brown, while those on the left lead up to Glaramara. The valley floor here is strewn with boulders, testament to the force of the beck when in flood. After heavy rainfall—and this area is prone to particularly high rain—it comes raging*

*down from the mountains, spreading out across the valley floor and depositing its load of rocks. In dry weather, it's sometimes hard to make out exactly where the beck is among all this debris.*

**2.** After crossing the humpback **Stockley Bridge**, go through a gate in a wall. Ignore the path to the left here (this forms part of the return route); instead, head straight up the well-trodden path. The gradient eases slightly as you pass beyond the tree-lined ravine that hides **Taylorgill Force**. Continue uphill beside **Styhead Gill**, crossing a footbridge just before you reach **Styhead Tarn**.

The clear path passes around the western side of the water.

*Lingmell dominates the scene straight ahead, the dark gash of Piers Gill slicing beneath its inhospitable eastern face.*

**3.** Before long you reach the Mountain Rescue stretcher box at Sty Head. Turn left here.

*Some of the Lake District's busiest paths converge at this pass. Sit here and watch the world go by: climbers making their way to Napes Needle, hikers intent on Great Gable's south-eastern breast, charity walkers struggling up England's highest mountain. It's like...well...Piccadilly Circus!*

At a faint fork in a short while, keep left—the path to the right is the popular Corridor Route to Scafell Pike. The loose, stony path climbs at a moderate angle to reach the edge of **Sprinkling Tarn**.

*Most walkers will stride on past Sprinkling Tarn, hardly giving it a second glance as they continue up to Esk Hause, but it's worth pausing for a while here. The tarn is cradled between the many lumps and bumps of Seathwaite Fell. The area is dotted with tiny pools*

*sparkling in hollows or hidden from view by encircling crags; and with superb views of the surrounding mountains, it's an excellent spot to explore at a leisurely pace. Those with the time and the energy can take a stroll out to Seathwaite Fell's northern summit with superb views down to Seathwaite and across to Skiddaw in the distance.*

**First light:** *Styhead Tarn remains in shadow as dawn reaches the surrounding fells, including Great Gable*

Continue along the clear Esk Hause path beyond the tarn, below the huge gullies that dissect Great End's magnificent northern buttresses.

**4.** About 350 metres beyond the tarn, as the rock beneath your feet turns red, turn left to cross the gill. Follow **Ruddy Gill** and then **Grains Gill** downstream on a clear path, with the slopes of Seathwaite Fell up to your left at first. The badly eroded path can be rather loose underfoot in places, but various attempts have been made to repair it

over the years. The many interesting gullies, waterfalls and pools in the gills help relieve the tedium of the relentless downhill slog.

**5.** You eventually cross Grains Gill on a narrow wooden bridge. Turn right at the next path junction, going through a gate to recross **Stockley Bridge**. Now retrace your steps to **Seathwaite** to complete the walk.

*On the way back into Seathwaite, you will see spoil heaps up on the slopes to the west. These belong to the now disused 'wad' mines. Wad is the local name for plumbago, more commonly known as*

*graphite. The discovery of graphite, early in the 16th century, gave rise, several hundred years later, to Keswick's famous pencil industry. According to local legend, it all started with a violent storm in Borrowdale,* *which led to trees being uprooted and the discovery of an unknown black material underneath. Shepherds then began using the mysterious substance to mark their sheep, creating the world's first pencils.* ♦

### Wet, wet, wet!

*Seathwaite is famous for being the wettest inhabited place in the country. The rain gauge that measures rainfall here is located near Sprinkling Tarn. The biggest downpour ever recorded during a 24-hour period in the UK was at Sprinkling Tarn in November 2009—a massive 314 millimetres, or more than one foot of rain. The deluge resulted in catastrophic flooding on the River Derwent in Keswick, Cockermouth and Workington.*

*Looking across Innominate Tarn to Great Gable*

# Innominate Tarn

*A stiff climb onto a popular fell surrounded by magnificent mountain scenery*

**What to expect:**
*Lakeshore paths, stony bridleway, rocky clamber, fell path*

**Distance/time:** 12.5km/7½ miles. Allow 3½-4½ hours

**Start:** National Park Pay and Display car park behind the Bridge Hotel in Buttermere

**Grid ref:** NY 174 169

**Ordnance Survey Map:** OL 4 *The English Lakes North-western area. Keswick, Cockermouth & Wigton*

**After the walk:** Croft House Café, Bridge Hotel and Fish Hotel, all in Buttermere

## Walk outline

*The easy walk beside Buttermere makes for a gentle warm-up for the climb onto Haystacks. After ascending to Scarth Gap, the route clambers up the fell's rocky western ridge. On the summit, a well-used path keeps to the northern edge of the fell, passing Innominate Tarn along the way. The descent uses a relatively quiet path on the southern side of Warnscale Beck and then returns via the lake.*

## Innominate Tarn

This pretty, reedy tarn is one of many bodies of water hidden among the maze of crags and heathery knolls that make up Haystacks. Viewed from the west, it reflects the iconic Great Gable; and, from the east, craggy Pillar. A favourite with guidebook writer Alfred Wainwright, it was here that his ashes were scattered after his death in 1991.

Although the route description keeps close to the northern edge of Haystacks, it is worth taking your time and going off-track occasionally to explore this complex but wonderful landscape.

*Haystacks' summit tarn*

*Wheatear*

## The Walk

**1.** Heading away from the main car park, turn right to follow the public bridleway to the left of the **Fish Hotel**—towards the lake. Passing through several gates and ignoring a path to Scale Bridge on the right, keep to this wide track as

**2.** As you draw level with the south-east end of the lake, leave the main path by bearing right to head towards a small conifer plantation. You are soon on the bridleway to Scarth Gap, linking the Buttermere valley with Ennerdale on the other side. As you ascend, don't be tempted to stay on the right-hand side of the wall that comes snaking steeply up from the valley below; you need to go through a gap soon after first encountering it. The path gets steeper and rougher underfoot as you toil uphill, until you finally reach **Scarth Gap**.

it winds its way to the lakeshore. After going through a gate providing access to the lake, turn right, soon crossing the outlet stream via a bridge. Cross a second bridge, go through the gate and then follow the lakeshore path. Whenever the route forks, keep left to enjoy spectacular views across **Buttermere**.

**Looking back:** *The view back to Buttermere from the path below Blackbeck Tarn*

**3.** Turn left at a large cairn to the left of the path in the pass. This marks the start of the climb onto Haystacks—a stony staircase that winds its way up the fellside. It becomes increasingly steep and rocky, and you may need to use your hands on the more difficult sections.

**4.** The first tarn you come to after the main climb is truly 'innominate', in that it is not marked and therefore remains unnamed on most maps. The actual **Innominate Tarn** lies a further 600 metres to the south-east—in a depression between rocky, heathery knolls. To reach it, keep to the path along the northern edge of the fell.

After passing to the left of Innominate Tarn, the path swings left to descend slightly. It then cuts beneath a dark crag before crossing **Blackbeck Tarn**'s outlet stream.

*Looking down the gully on the left here, there is a spectacular view to the green valley below, including Buttermere and Crummock Water.*

**Wainwright's favourite:** *High Crag from the unnamed tarn on the top of Haystacks*

Beyond the outlet stream, the path climbs again and then passes round the side of **Green Crag**. It is soon joined by another path and then crosses some damp ground. Before long, you will see a less well-used path to the right, heading off at a right angle to the main track. Our route swings left here, aiming, it seems, directly for the quarry workings on Fleetwith in the distance.

**5.** When the track then swings right again, leave it by turning left along a narrow path to begin the descent. This winds its way steadily to **Warnscale Bottom**, passing **Warnscale Bothy** along the way and cutting beneath Haystacks' dark, northern cliffs. Cross the sturdy bridge over **Warnscale Beck** and follow the faint path up to a clear bridleway, along which you bear left.

**6.** Turn left at the road, soon passing **Gatesgarth Farm**, one of the largest privately-owned farms in the National Park. When you reach the lakeshore again, take the gravel path off to the left. This makes its way along the lakeshore, back towards the village, passing through a short, dark tunnel cut into the rock along the way.

**7.** On reaching the western end of the lake, go through a small gate and keep straight ahead. The path goes through a series of gates and passes between the buildings of **Wilkinsyke Farm** to reach the road just below tiny St James' Church in **Buttermere**. Turn left and then left again at the Bridge Hotel. Continue to the car park on the right to complete the walk. ♦

### The 'Beauty of Buttermere'

*The Fish Hotel was once home to Mary Robinson, the 'Beauty of Buttermere'. Praised in an early guide book, she was subsequently seduced by and married Colonel Alexander Hope, MP for Linlithgow. Sadly, soon after the wedding it was discovered that the real Colonel Hope was overseas. Mary had married an imposter—John Hatfield, wanted for forgery and bigamy. He was later arrested and hanged for his crimes.*

*Angle Tarn bathed in dawn light*

# Angle Tarn

*A moderate walk to a tranquil tarn with great views of the Helvellyn range*

**What to expect:**
*Rough tracks and fell paths, which may be wet in places*

**Distance/time:** 9.5km/6 miles. Allow 3-4 hours

**Start:** A small free parking area at the eastern end of Hartsop. There is alternative parking about a kilometre away, at Cow Bridge on the A592, near Brothers Water

**Grid ref:** NY 410 131

**Ordnance Survey Map:** OL 5 *The English Lakes North-eastern area. Penrith, Patterdale & Caldbeck*

**After the walk:** The Brotherswater Inn, 1.5km south of Hartsop

## Walk outline

*The initial climb beside the waterfalls of Hayeswater Gill is fairly gentle. From Hayeswater itself, though, it steepens and crosses damp ground to reach a high point of 556 metres near Satura Crag. With fantastic views west, a good path drops to Angle Tarn and then Boredale Hause. A rough track leads back into the valley where the walk ends with a quiet trail through ancient woods.*

## Angle Tarn

There are two Angle Tarns in the Lake District: one at the foot of Esk Pike and this one in the eastern fells, close to Ullswater. It is exquisitely located at 479 metres above sea level, tucked in at the base of Angletarn Pikes. On the route of Wainwright's Coast to Coast Walk, it's a popular spot with wild campers who wake to the glorious scene of Fairfield, St Sunday Crag and the Helvellyn range lit up by the morning sun.

As well as superb views, the walk provides plenty of interest, including a visit to one of the Lake District's prettiest hamlets.

*Track to Hayeswater*

*Sundew*

## The Walk

**1.** Go through the gate at the far end of the car park and walk along the clear track—signposted to 'Hayeswater'. After crossing a cattle grid, the track forks. Bear right and descend to **Hayeswater Gill**, crossing via a bridge.

*It's hard to imagine it now, but this used to be a busy lead mining area. The scant remains of Low Hartsop mine are visible nearby, at the confluence of Hayeswater Gill and Pasture Beck. Stone piers and a wheel pit are all that remain of a huge water wheel constructed to drain the mine, which suffered badly from flooding. The works were abandoned in 1878.*

**2.** The wide, stony track climbs beside Hayeswater Gill, with several delightful waterfalls inevitably drawing your attention. On reaching **Hayeswater reservoir**, beautifully located in a bowl between Gray Crag and the Straits of Rigindale, cross the outlet stream via the bridge near the dam.

**3.** Just after crossing the tumbledown wall on the other side of the bridge, the stony path turns to grass and you are presented with a three-way split. Bear left here, climbing fairly steeply on grass, soon with a drystone wall over to your left.

**4.** At a junction of paths, turn left, quickly crossing the wall. Things might get a little boggy underfoot

**Bright and early:** *The sun's first rays illuminate Angle Tarn*

in places now, the peat stripped bare of surface vegetation by the combined actions of water and walkers' boots.

*You are now on the route of Alfred Wainwright's Coast to Coast Walk from St Bees on Cumbria's coast to Robin Hood's Bay on the North Yorkshire coast. The famous guidebook writer devised this 190-mile route in 1973. Crossing some of England's most beautiful scenery, including three National Parks, it is now one of the most popular long-distance walks in the world.*

As you wind your way through an area of rocky outcrops near **Satura Crag**, keep close to the drystone wall/fence that recently came in from the left.

*The views to the west, which have been gradually improving since you left the reservoir, are now absolutely superb. The amazing panorama of mountains includes Hart Crag, the dark, eastern cliffs of Fairfield, St Sunday Crag and the Helvellyn range. Take some time to enjoy the views to the east too—the long line of misty hills that can be seen in the distance from time to time is the Pennines.*

**Revealed:** *Beyond Angle Tarn, the narrow path gives superb views across to Deepdale, Fairfield and the Helvellyn range*

**5.** Just after going through a gap in a drystone wall, you will see **Angle Tarn** below. Ignoring any trails to the right, keep to the clear path as it descends to the water and then swings left to ascend slightly. The ground on your left now suddenly drops away, revealing jaw-dropping views down the steep slopes into the upper reaches of Patterdale and across to lonely Deepdale. This superb path hugs the edge of the fell and then drops into a shallow gap between the hills.

**6.** Having crossed a small beck on stepping stones, you reach a flat, grassy area at **Boredale Hause**. Continue in roughly the same direction to pick up a descending track that immediately splits in two. Bear left here. This track is steep and loose in its early stages, but things improve as you descend.

**7.** Bear left at a track junction close to the valley bottom. Just before you reach the bridge over **Angletarn Beck**, bear left up a faint path heading towards the beck. Ford it just a few metres upstream of the bridge. On the other side of the small gate, keep to the clearest path at all times. After an area of woodland, the

path all but disappears in the mud, but persevere: head up the tiny outcrop of rock and you will pick it up again as it passes beneath a small crag and then through a gate. Turn left along the vehicle track, which climbs briefly before dropping down into **Hartsop**. Turn left along the lane and walk through the hamlet. Return to the car park to complete the walk. ♦

### Red deer

*These fells are home to England's oldest native herd of red deer, said to be the only herd that hasn't cross-bred with sika deer. The ancient deer forest itself is centred on The Nab.*

*In autumn, listen for the deep roaring of the stags in rut. These enormous males, who congregate in single-sex herds for much of the year, have now gone their separate ways and are gathering their harems for the mating season.*

*Red Tarn and Swirral Edge*

# Red Tarn

*Magnificent views of valleys and fells on this outstanding walk to a high mountain tarn*

**Distance/time:** 10.5km/6½ miles. Allow 3½-4½ hours

**Start:** Main National Park Pay and Display car park in Glenridding

**Grid ref:** NY 386 169

**Ordnance Survey Map:** OL 5 *The English Lakes North-eastern area. Penrith, Patterdale & Caldbeck*

**After the walk:** Choice of pubs and cafés in Glenridding

## Walk outline

*The climb to Red Tarn is long, but the climbing is well spaced-out, with only one or two steep sections. The paths as far as Lanty's Tarn are well walked, but the next section of the ascent is on a wonderful, little-used trail with superb views up Grisedale. Constructed paths lead from the ridge to Red Tarn and down to Glenridding Beck. A delightful leat route, hugging the side of the fell high above the valley floor, then takes you most of the way back to Glenridding.*

*Grisedale*

## Red Tarn

Red Tarn is spectacularly situated at the bottom of the cliffs of Helvellyn's east face, cradled between the mountain's two famous arêtes, Striding Edge and Swirral Edge. At 718 metres above sea level, it's the sixth highest tarn in the Lake District and home to brown trout and the rare schelly.

Taking in the impressive Grisedale and Glenridding valleys, the walk is pure delight from beginning to end—using excellent paths with fantastic views of the surrounding craggy mountains.

*Raven*

## The Walk

**1.** From the car park, head back out onto the main road and turn right. Turn right again along a surfaced lane immediately after crossing the bridge over **Glenridding Beck**. Bear left at a fork in the track—towards Lanty's Tarn. As you draw level with a pair of cottages, turn left at a small sign that reads 'Grisedale, Lanty's Tarn, Helvellyn, either path'.

The route crosses a small bridge, goes through a gate and then swings right to climb through the woods, soon joined by the alternative path coming up from the right. The next gate provides access

to bracken-covered slopes and you now have a superb view across the valley to your right. The path forks just before another small gate. Bear left here, away from the gate.

**2.** You soon go through a larger wooden gate to access **Lanty's Tarn**, a calm stretch of water surrounded by trees. Continue on the path beside the tarn. When the trees on your right end, you will see a faint path going off to the right, along the edge of the woods. Ignore this, but a few strides further on, take a second path to the right (south-west), soon looking across to St Sunday Crag.

Another path comes up from the left and, together, they make their way over

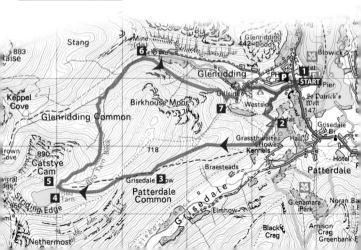

**Mountain cirque:** *Looking down on Red Tarn from Striding Edge, on Helvellyn*

to a small area of woodland. Enter via a tall gate. Once out the other side, bear right at a fork, heading uphill. Keep right at the next fork too, staying with the higher path with excellent views straight up Grisedale. The way ahead briefly becomes less obvious after a gate/stile; but keep heading west and the route soon becomes clearer again.

Down to the left is the well-worn path that leads from Patterdale to Striding Edge. You will eventually drop down to

this, but for now delight in the seclusion of this higher path and its views.

**3.** After joining the main path, follow it uphill. When you reach the ridge, do not cross the stepped stile in the wall up to the left; instead, climb the ladder stile in front of you. On the other side, take the path directly ahead, heading away from the wall—straight towards **Helvellyn.**

**4. Red Tarn** is hidden from view from the main path. To reach the water's edge, bear left when the constructed track negotiates its way through a slightly rockier area.

**Cradled:** *Red Tarn with Striding Edge on one side and Swirral Edge on the other*

*Sitting at the foot of England's third highest mountain, this is a great place to rest and watch the walkers on Striding Edge up to the left. There have been many accidents, many of them fatal, along this narrow arête over the years. The exit from the ridge, in fact, is marked by a plaque telling the story of artist Charles Gough, whose body was found in 1805 at the base of the crags beneath this spot. His rotting remains had been guarded for three months by his dog.*

**5.** When you cross the outlet stream, bear right, away from the tarn, and rejoin the main path, which swings left. A few metres later, at a fork, turn right. You now begin descending along a clear, wide track. About 1.8 kilometres from the tarn, cross **Red Tarn Beck** via a small, wooden bridge and then continue with **Glenridding Beck** on your left.

**6.** About 200 metres after passing and ignoring a bridge over the beck, you will see a faint, grassy path off to the left. Ignore this. Instead, stay on the clear, level path that follows the line of a disused leat. Do not leave this until you

come to a wall apparently blocking your way ahead. Bear left here to descend a rocky path. At the bottom of the short descent, turn right.

**7.** Cross a ladder stile beside a gate and follow the track down to a lane. Turn left and then turn right along a wide track just before the bridge across the beck. This leads back into **Glenridding village** to complete the walk. ♦

### Greenside Mine

*Lead was discovered at Greenside in the 17th century, but serious development didn't begin until 1822. By 1849, there were 300 workers here, making it the largest lead mine in England. It was the first mine in Britain to use electrical winding, generating its own electricity with water turbines. The rushing water was supplied by the damming of tarns. The mine closed in 1962.*

*The path down to Bowscale Tarn*

# Bowscale Tarn

*A steep ascent but an otherwise moderate walk on the
lonely moorland of the Northern Fells*

**What to expect:**
*Tracks; grassy paths, wet
in valley and indistinct
on fells; loose slate on
ascent*

**Distance/time:** 10km/6½ miles. Allow 3-4 hours

**Start:** Bowscale Moss parking area just south of Mosedale, near
Mungrisdale

**Grid ref:** NY 359 316

**Ordnance Survey Map:** OL 5  *The English Lakes North-eastern area.
Penrith, Patterdale & Caldbeck*

**After the walk:** Mill Inn at Mungrisdale

## Walk outline

*After a short section on a road, the route heads into the hills
at Mungrisdale. It follows the River Glenderamackin upstream
before heading out along a grassy spur to Bannerdale Crags'
eastern ridge. A steep, but uncomplicated climb ensues,
followed by an opportunity to stride out over the top of these
broad-backed, empty hills. After dropping steeply to Bowscale
Tarn, a good track leads back to the road.*

## Bowscale Tarn

Once popular with Victorian tourists, Bowscale Tarn is silent
now, an oasis of solitude and serenity in a National Park
that receives over 15 million visitors each year. Hardly ever
seeing the sun in winter, it hides in a perfect glacial bowl
at the foot of Bowscale Fell and is ringed on one side by
moody cliffs.

*River Glenderamackin*

This walk drops onto this atmospheric spot from above,
from the lofty moorland of the lonely Northern Fells,
having first climbed via a chink in the mile-long line of dark
cliffs that make up Bannerdale Crags.

*Buzzard*

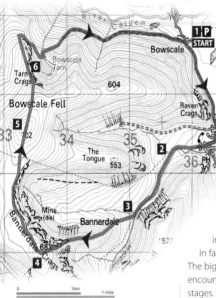

## The Walk

**1.** From the parking area, walk south along the minor road into **Mungrisdale**. After entering the village, turn right along a rough track beside a 'phone box. The wide track goes through a large gate and heads towards the hills.

**2.** About 40 metres after crossing a bridge, turn left along a sometimes muddy path beside the **River Glenderamackin**.

**3.** Having walked upstream for one kilometre, you ford **Bannerdale Beck**. Turn right immediately, along a narrow path climbing the steep embankment. The faint path leads onto a short stretch of low, grassy ridge and then to the foot of **Bannerdale Crags**. The route up the front of the fell looks intimidating as you stand at the bottom looking at the dark cliffs and shattered rock above, but first impressions can be deceiving. In fact, it presents few difficulties. The biggest problem you are likely to encounter is loose slate in the early stages. After that, the trick is to keep close to the rocks on the right. It's steep and occasionally stony, but there's no scrambling involved.

**4.** As you come out of the climb, the path swings right to reach a cairn. Follow the clear path along the eastern edge of the fell. This heads north-north-west at first. As it begins to swing north-north-east, bear left along a faint, easy-to-miss path. This runs almost parallel with the rim path at first, but then makes more directly for the shelter on top of **Bowscale Fell**.

**Mountain pool:** *Bowscale Tarn is cradled by fells*

**5.** From the summit cairn, there are two paths heading down the other side of the fell. Take the less distinct one to the left. As the path swings north-north-west, it approaches the edge of steep ground dropping down to Bowscale Tarn to the right. The route eventually descends this steep ground, but not until **Tarn Crags** has been bypassed. Only as the path ahead becomes even less distinct should you turn right and begin your descent on a clear path.

**6.** Having dropped to **Bowscale Tarn**, cross the outlet stream and turn left on the clear path. This leads back to the minor road where the walk started. At the end of the track, return to the parking area to complete the walk. ♦

### Fell ponies

*Fell ponies wander the road between Bowscale and Mungrisdale. These friendly creatures trace their history back to the Romans, when indigenous ponies bred with those introduced by the occupiers. In the 13th century, with the rise of the wool trade, they began to be used as pack animals. Come the Industrial Revolution, they carried lead and iron ore from the fells to the smelting works on the north-east coast.*

# Useful Information

## Cumbria Tourism

Cumbria Tourism's official website covers everything from accommodation and events to attractions and adventure. **www.golakes.co.uk**

## Lake District National Park

The Lake District National Park website also has information on things to see and do, plus maps, webcams and news. **www.lakedistrict.gov.uk**

## Tourist Information Centres

The main TICs provide free information on everything from accommodation and travel to what's on and walking advice.

| | | |
|---|---|---|
| Ambleside | 01539 432 582 | tic@thehubofambleside.com |
| Bowness | 01539 442 895 | bownesstic@lake-district.gov.uk |
| Coniston | 01539 441 533 | mail@conistontic.org |
| Keswick | 01768 772 645 | keswicktic@lake-district.gov.uk |
| Penrith | 01768 867 466 | pen.tic@eden.gov.uk |
| Ullswater | 01768 482 414 | ullswatertic@lake-district.gov.uk |
| Windermere | 01539 446 499 | windermeretic@southlakeland.gov.uk |

## Emergencies

The Lake District is covered by twelve volunteer mountain rescue teams. In a real emergency:

**1.** Make a note of your location (with OS grid reference, if possible); the name, age and sex of the casualty; their injuries; how many people are in the group; and your mobile phone number.

**2.** Dial 999 or 112 and ask for the Cumbria police, and then for Mountain Rescue.

**3.** Give them your prepared details.

**4.** Do NOT change position until contacted by the mountain rescue team.

## Weather

Five day forecast for the Lake District
0844 846 2444          **www.lakedistrict.gov.uk/weatherline**